WHO'S HOO? OWLS!

Screech Owls

by Rachael Barnes

BLASTOFF! READERS 2

BELLWETHER MEDIA • MINNEAPOLIS, MN

Blastoff! Readers are carefully developed by literacy experts to build reading stamina and move students toward fluency by combining standards-based content with developmentally appropriate text.

Level 1 provides the most support through repetition of high-frequency words, light text, predictable sentence patterns, and strong visual support.

Level 2 offers early readers a bit more challenge through varied sentences, increased text load, and text-supportive special features.

Level 3 advances early-fluent readers toward fluency through increased text load, less reliance on photos, advancing concepts, longer sentences, and more complex special features.

★ Blastoff! Universe

This edition first published in 2025 by Bellwether Media, Inc.

Library of Congress Cataloging-in-Publication Data

Names: Barnes, Rachael, author.
Title: Screech owls / by Rachael Barnes.
Description: Minneapolis, MN : Bellwether Media, Inc., 2025. | Series: Blastoff! Readers: who's hoo? Owls! | Includes bibliographical references and index. | Audience: Ages 5-8 | Audience: Grades 2-3 | Summary: "Relevant images match informative text in this introduction to screech owls. Intended for students in kindergarten through third grade"-- Provided by publisher.
Identifiers: LCCN 2024000760 (print) | LCCN 2024000761 (ebook) | ISBN 9798886879803 (library binding) | ISBN 9781644879122 (ebook)
Subjects: LCSH: Screech owls--Juvenile literature.
Classification: LCC QL696.S83 B37 2025 (print) | LCC QL696.S83 (ebook) | DDC 598.9/7--dc23/eng/20240123
LC record available at https://lccn.loc.gov/2024000760
LC ebook record available at https://lccn.loc.gov/2024000761

Editor: Christina Leaf Series Designer: Brittany McIntosh Book Designer: Veah Demmin

Printed in the United States of America, North Mankato, MN.

Table of Contents

Tree Bark or Feathers?

eastern screech owl

Screech owls live in North and South America. One of the most common **species** is the eastern screech owl.

These owls like forests with many trees.

Screech owls only grow to around 10 inches (25 centimeters) tall. They are small owls.

Their **wingspan** reaches up to 2 feet (0.6 meters) wide.

Eastern Screech Owl Wingspan

up to 2 feet (0.6 meters) wide

Screech owls can have gray, brown, or reddish feathers. Their feathers look like tree bark!

They have darker feathers
on the sides of their faces.

Screech owls have short tails and rounded wings. **Ear tufts** poke out from their square heads.

Their beaks and **talons** are sharp!

Spot a Screech Owl!

Diving in the Dark

At night, screech owls wait on low **perches**. They look and listen for **prey**.

They dive silently toward their food.

Screech owls mostly eat birds, **insects**, and small **mammals**.

Screech Owl Food

birds

insects

small mammals

They grab some prey out of the air with their sharp talons!

Screech owls hide from larger owls and other **predators**.

When screech owls see danger, they stand tall and flat against a tree. They almost perfectly blend in!

Singing Pairs

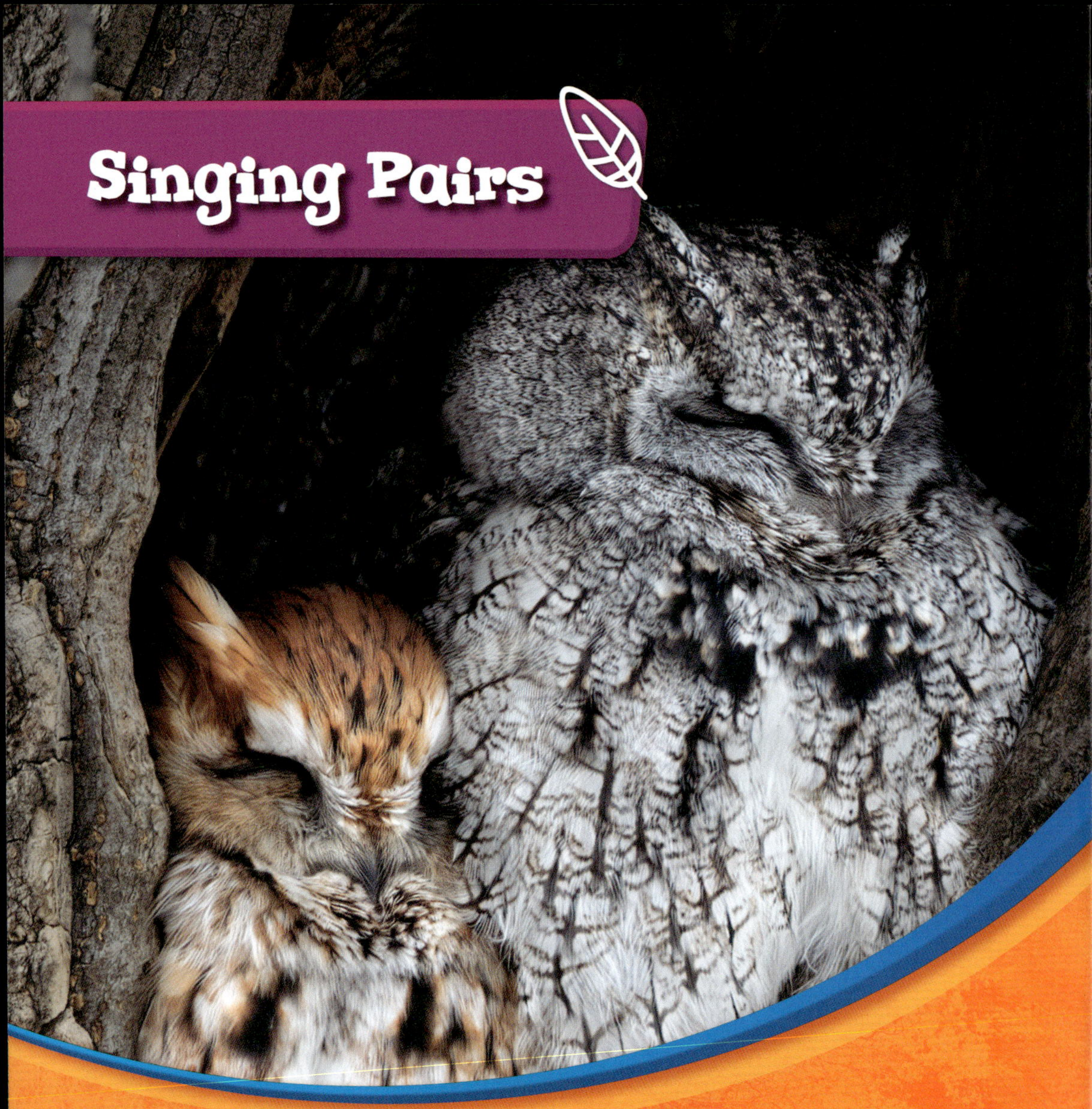

Screech owls often rest in tree holes during the day. These owls live in pairs.

The owls **mate** in early spring. They sing together!

Females lay two to six eggs. **Owlets** come out of their eggs in about four weeks.

Soon, they become **fledglings**. They learn to fly!

Growing Up

1 

egg

4 to 5 weeks

2 

owlet

4 weeks

3 

fledgling

5 to 10 weeks

life span: up to 14 years

Glossary

ear tufts—feathers on the heads of screech owls; ear tufts are not used for hearing.

fledglings—young owls that have feathers for flight

insects—small animals with six legs and hard outer bodies; an insect's body is divided into three parts.

mammals—warm-blooded animals that have backbones and feed their young milk

mate—to join together to make young

owlets—baby owls

perches—places to sit or rest above the ground

predators—animals that hunt other animals for food

prey—animals that are hunted by other animals for food

species—kinds of animals

talons—the strong, sharp claws of owls and other raptors

wingspan—the distance from the tip of one wing to the tip of the other wing

To Learn More

AT THE LIBRARY

Barnes, Rachael. *Saw-whet Owls*. Minneapolis, Minn.: Bellwether Media, 2025.

Porter, Jane. *So You Want to Be an Owl*. Somerville, Mass.: Candlewick Press, 2021.

Wilson, Mark. *Owling: Enter the World of the Mysterious Birds of the Night*. North Adams, Mass.: Storey Publishing, 2019.

ON THE WEB

FACTSURFER

Factsurfer.com gives you a safe, fun way to find more information.

1. Go to www.factsurfer.com.
2. Enter "screech owls" into the search box and click 🔍.
3. Select your book cover to see a list of related content.

Index

The images in this book are reproduced through the courtesy of: Harry Collins Photography, front cover (screech owl); Malachi Jacobs, background; mlorenz, p. 3; Leena Robinson, p. 4; Rena Schild, p. 6; Joe McDonald, p. 7; Greg Meland, pp. 8, 23; My Generations Art, p. 9; Jack Nevitt, p. 10; CampCrazy Photography, p. 11; Tony Campbell, p. 12; Troy Lim, pp. 12–13; Chase D'animulls, pp. 14–15; Jeff W. Jarrett, p. 15 (birds); Jay Ondreicka, p. 15 (insects); jitkagold, p. 15 (small mammals); Tomas Drahos, p. 16; Christopher MacDonald, p. 17; lavin photography, p. 18; Grindstone Media Group, p. 19; LagunaticPhoto, pp. 20, 21 (egg); Avalon / Universal Images Group / Getty Images, pp. 20–21; Weber, p. 21 (owlet); FotoRequest, p. 21 (fledgling).